W9-BFC-159

Why Do Kittens PURR?

For Norma Fox Mazer —M. D. B.

To Quinn, with love —H. C.

SIMON & SCHUSTER BOOKS FOR YOUNG READERS
An imprint of Simon & Schuster Children's Publishing Division
1230 Avenue of the Americas, New York, New York 10020
Text copyright © 2003 by Marion Dane Bauer
Illustrations copyright © 2003 by Henry Cole
All rights reserved, including the right of reproduction in whole or in part in
any form.
SIMON & SCHUSTER BOOKS FOR YOUNG READERS is a trademark of Simon &
Schuster.
Book design by Mark Siegel
The text for this book is set in Steam.
The illustrations are rendered in acrylic paints and colored pencil.
Manufactured in China
10 9 8 7 6 5 4 3 2 1
Library of Congress Cataloging-in-Publication Data
Bauer, Marion Dane.
Why do kittens purr? / by Marion Dane Bauer ; illustrated by Henry Cole.—
1st ed.
p. cm.
Summary: Simple rhymes tell why kittens, bears, kangaroos, and other
animals behave the way they do.
ISBN 0-689-84179-5
[1. Animals—Habits and behavior—Fiction. 2. Stories in rhyme.] I. Cole,
Henry, ill. II. Title.
PZ8.3.B3199 Wh 2003
[E]—dc21   2001042974

Why Do Kittens PURR?

by Marion Dane Bauer
illustrated by Henry Cole

Simon & Schuster Books for Young Readers
New York London Toronto Sydney Singapore

Why do kittens purr?
Because they're happy,
deep inside their fur.

Why do puppies pat their paws,
raise their rumps,
twirl their tails?

To say,
"Let's play!"

What makes lions roar?

They want more.
And more.
And more.
And more!

Why do spiders spin?
To make a plate
to keep their dinner in.

Why do rabbits
sit like stone?

To disappear
when you come near.
If you see them anyway?
They'll run, run, run away.

Why do mice squeak?
To say, "I'm shy.
Please, don't peek!"

What song do robins sing in spring?
"This day is fine.
This nest, this tree, this world
are mine!"

Why do wolves cry, "Owoo~oo~oo"?

To say, "We're over here.
Where are you~ou~ou?"

What makes frogs
hop, hop, hop?

They can't stop, stop, stop.

And kangaroos,
why do they hop too?

It's what their mamas
taught them to do.

So why do bees buzz?
Just because!

What makes bears sleep so long?

The snow tucks them in.
And the wind sings them a song.

Why does the moon peek
in your window at night?

To say, "I'm here.
Everything's all right."

And why does the sun come back
when night is through?

To see *you*.
To see *you*!